RELATIVIDAD
Relativity

Written by / Escrito por **Michael Smith**

Illustrated by / Ilustrado por **Octavio Oliva**

East West Discovery Press

Manhattan Beach, California

The sky is high,

El cielo es alto,

2

the trees are low.

los árboles son bajos.

The trees are high,

Los árboles son altos,

4

the grass is low.

el pasto es bajo.

The grass is high,

El pasto es alto,

the ants are low.

las hormigas son bajas.

What is high,

¿Qué es alto?

and what is low?

¿Qué es bajo?

Planes go fast,

Los aviones van rápido,

and cars go slow.

y los autos van lento.

Cars go fast,

Los autos van rápido,

12

Kids go fast,
and snails go slow.

Los niños van rápido,
y los caracoles van lento.

And snails go fast,
and trees grow slow.

Los caracoles van rápido,
y los árboles crecen lento.

Trees grow slow,
don't you know?

Los árboles crecen lento,
¡qué estupendo!

16

Trees grow high,
oh my, oh my.

Los árboles crecen alto,
sin sobresaltos.

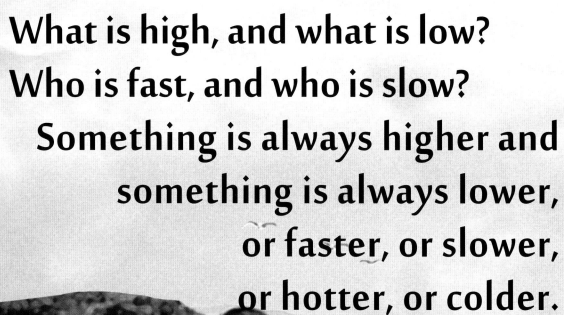

What is high, and what is low?
Who is fast, and who is slow?
Something is always higher and
something is always lower,
or faster, or slower,
or hotter, or colder.

ICECREAM

¿Qué es alto y qué es bajo?
¿Quién va lento y quién va rápido?
Siempre hay algo más alto y
siempre algo más bajo,
o más rápido, o más lento,
o menos rico o más suculento.

And those are the facts.
As you can see, it is all about
Relativity.

Las cosas son así,
con toda seguridad.
Todo tiene que ver con la...

IVIDAD

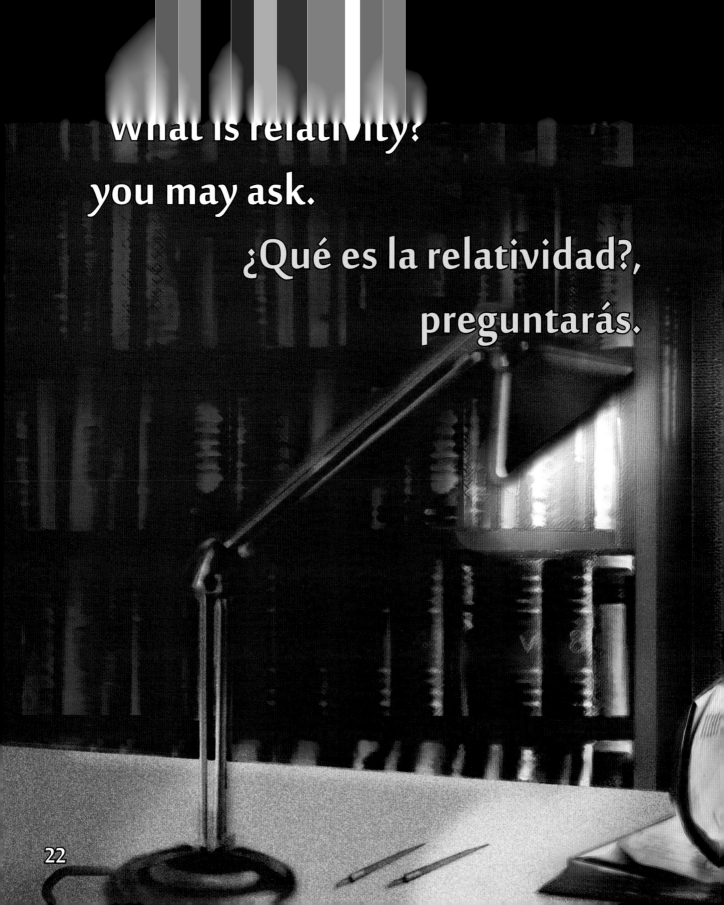

What is relativity?
you may ask.

¿Qué es la relatividad?,
preguntarás.

Finding out should be your task.

Si quieres saberlo, lo averiguarás.

There is no high,
there is no low,

No hay algo alto
ni hay algo bajo,

24

just levels of something
taller or below.

sólo niveles de arriba abajo.

If you think going
to China is far,

Si crees que China
queda lejos,

what would you think about
going to a star?
¿y las estrellas del universo?

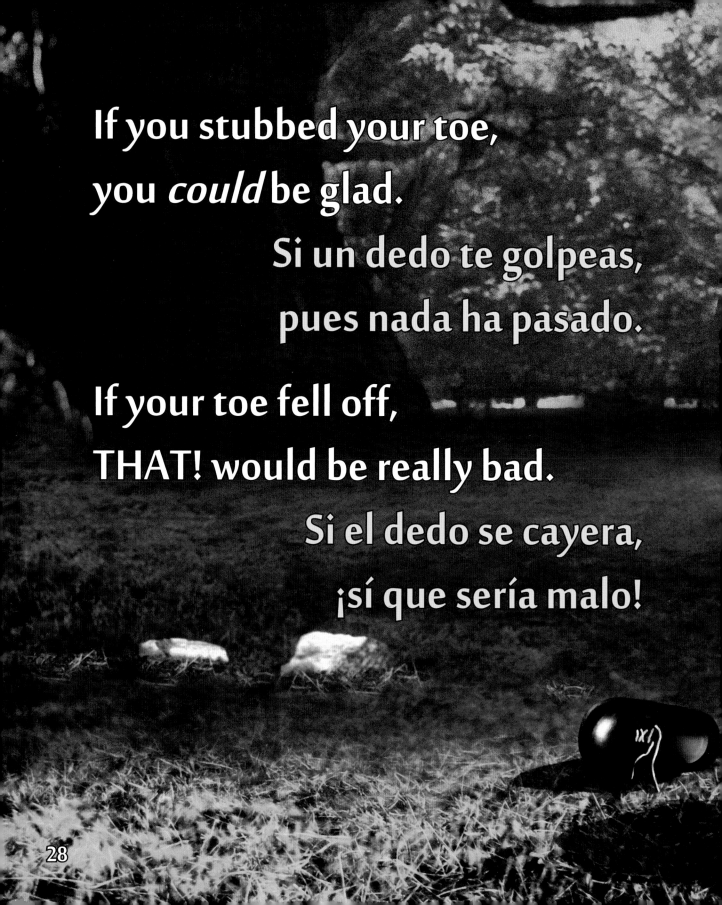

If you stubbed your toe,
you *could* be glad.

Si un dedo te golpeas,
pues nada ha pasado.

If your toe fell off,
THAT! would be really bad.

Si el dedo se cayera,
¡sí que sería malo!

So, the next time you look at
something good, or bad,
or fast, or slow,

Por eso, si alguna vez,
algo malo o bueno ves,

or anything you can see,
just think a thought about
RELATIVITY.

o lento o veloz tal vez,
esto no es casualidad, es la
RELATIVIDAD.

For kids who know that the world is not simply black and white.
—Michael Smith

To my loving wife, Vianney, and our son, Oliver.
—Octavio Oliva

Text copyright © 2011 by Michael Smith
Illustrations copyright © 2011 by East West Discovery Press
Spanish translation copyright © 2011 by East West Discovery Press

Published by East West Discovery Press
P.O. Box 3585, Manhattan Beach, CA 90266
Phone: 310-545-3730, Fax: 310-545-3731
Website: www.eastwestdiscovery.com

Written by Michael Smith
Illustrated by Octavio Oliva
Spanish translation by Redactores en Red
Edited by Marcie Rouman
Design and production by Icy Smith and Jennifer Thomas

Library of Congress Cataloging-in-Publication Data
Smith, Michael, 1961-
    Relativity = Relatividad / written by/escrito por Michael Smith ; illustrated by/ilustrado por Octavio Oliva. -- 1st bilingual English and Spanish ed.
        p. cm.
    ISBN 978-0-9832278-3-0 (hardcover : alk. paper) 1. Relativity--Juvenile poetry. 2. Children's poetry, American. I. Oliva, Octavio, 1976- ill. II. Title. III. Title: Relatividad.
    PS3619.M59223R45 2011
    811'.6--dc22

                                                                                2011021813

ISBN-13: 978-0-9832278-3-0 Hardcover
First Bilingual English and Spanish Edition 2011
Printed in China
Published in the United States of America